Sent To Serve
The Chaplains of 9/11

Wally Johnston

Copyright © 2011 Wally Johnston

All rights reserved.

ISBN:1461074266
ISBN-13:978-1461074267

DEDICATION

This book is dedicated to the men and women who serve as public safety chaplains everywhere, to their spouses, families, and places of worship that make their service possible.

"I can't begin to tell you how much I appreciate what the chaplains did for us. I hope this book will provide you as much peace as the chaplains gave."

Officer Arnold Chow
79th Precinct, NYPD

CONTENTS

	Acknowledgments	i
	Introduction	1
1	The 9/11 Call	9
2	The 9/11 Heart	22
3	The 9/11 Cost	46
4	The 9/11 Reward	61
5	The 9/11 Hope	67
6	The Chaplain In The Local Community	77
	Conclusion	83
	About The Author	85

ACKNOWLEDGMENTS

I would like to thank the following chaplains for their contributions to this work:

Ray Baker: Elmore County, Alabama Sheriff's Office; Jim Cox: Wythe County, Virginia Sheriff's Office; Joe D'Angelo: Port Authority Police Dept. of New York & New Jersey; ATF; Nassau County, New York Police Department; New York State Chaplain, FOB; William Glennie: Arizona Dept. of Public Safety; U.S. Marshal's Service; Arizona Highway Patrol; FBI; Maricopa County, Arizona Sheriff's Office; Jan Heglund: San Rafael, California Police Department; Robert Johnson: ATF; Waynesboro, Virginia Police Department; Steve Lee: Peace Officer Ministries; David Owens: Johnson County, Indiana Sheriff's Office; Indianapolis International Airport; Indiana National Guard Reserve; Beth Wilson: Spokane, Washington Police Department.

My thanks to Chaplain Russ Guppy, Tacoma, Washington Police Department, without whose encouragement I would have missed my Ground Zero experience.

Thank you to the police departments who allowed me the privilege to serve with them: Santa Monica, CA; Abingdon, IL; Beaverton, OR; Sherwood, OR.

To the brave men and women of the Port Authority Police Department (PAPD), New York Police Department (NYPD), and the Fire Department of New York (FDNY).

To my wife, Linda, and my friends Phil & Donna Yount for their proofreading services.

INTRODUCTION

"It is my strong belief that when people are blessed to experience something profound, they inherit the responsibility to share that with those for whom they care. That would be my time at Ground Zero...and you."

Rev. Jan Heglund -- Chaplain, San Rafael, CA Police Department

In the movie, "Pearl Harbor," there is a quote made by Col. Doolittle on the aircraft carrier USS Hornet. They were on a secret mission to bomb Japan after the December 7, 1941 attack at Pearl Harbor. Alec Baldwin, who plays Doolittle, knows there is a great possibility that some of these men may not return from this mission. He turns to a staff member and says, "There's nothing stronger than the heart of a volunteer."

As we approach the tenth anniversary of 9/11, many Americans will reflect on the events of that day without realizing the extent of the volunteer effort that helped pull us through those difficult days. One such group is the public safety chaplains who converged upon those tragic scenes. Let's face it, many people don't even know public safety chaplains exist let alone what they do. One needs only to ask the folks at the New York Fire Department (FDNY). One of their five chaplains, Father Mychal Judge, was the first recorded death in the collapse of the Twin Towers of the World Trade Center on September 11, 2001.

Millions of people saw the photograph of Chaplain Mychal Judge being carried away from the rubble of the towers. They heard the word "chaplain" associated to his name but many had little knowledge of that word. I was a law enforcement chaplain for over 25 years. It didn't take long for me to figure out that many people don't know what chaplains do or even what a chaplain *is*. This was reinforced the other day at a coffee shop. I had been speaking to the twenty-something year old barista and the owner about my book. When I showed her the web page with the photo of the Portland, Oregon chaplains at Ground Zero, she had the classic "deer-in-the-headlights" stare. She had no concept of chaplaincy. I hope reading this book will introduce you to that concept and help you better understand what chaplains do every day through the "window" of 9/11. To get us started, a chaplain is a man or woman committed to being an emotional and spiritual resource to a specific group, i.e. police, fire, military, hospital. There are some chaplains who do not serve as a spiritual resource. This book is about those who do.

Volunteers from around this country and the world came to New York to help after the World Trade Center attack. Many of them worked in the respite centers, offering aid to those who worked on the "pile" (the heaped up remains of the World Trade Center). They volunteered through various humanitarian groups, church organizations, and public safety agencies. They were college students from Pennsylvania, construction workers from Chicago, and housewives from New England. They served food and refreshments and provided rest and encouragement. One of the centers I frequented was St. Paul's Chapel, just down the street from the World Trade Center. Many back massages were given to public safety personnel just feet away from the box seat that President George Washington used for worship. Exhausted workers slept in the pews. I have returned since 9/11. St. Paul's is now a shrine that many visit when they tour Ground Zero.

On September 11, 2001, there were many heroes who wore uniforms or fire turnouts (outer protective clothing), who climbed the stairs of the World Trade Center. They saved lives and lost many of their own in the effort. Chaplains are like the public safety people who run into towers while others are rushing out. They rush into others' lives that have been destroyed by tragedy and provide comfort and care to the victims and those who assist them.

Hundreds of chaplains responded to assist the men and women of public safety who lost so much that September day. Two of the chaplains in our group responded to serve a week's shift at Ground Zero one month after the attack. When they returned, they told others of us we had to go back with them, the need was so great. I'm not much for travel but I thought I could contribute in another way—through the gift of writing. We were told the Port Authority Police were lost in the shadows of the NYPD and FDNY, yet the World Trade Center was their headquarters and jurisdiction. I decided to write a booklet of support. About 600 copies of *A Special Message to the Port Authority Police of New York and New Jersey* were printed and distributed, thanks to the generosity of a local Christian school. (See photo next page.)

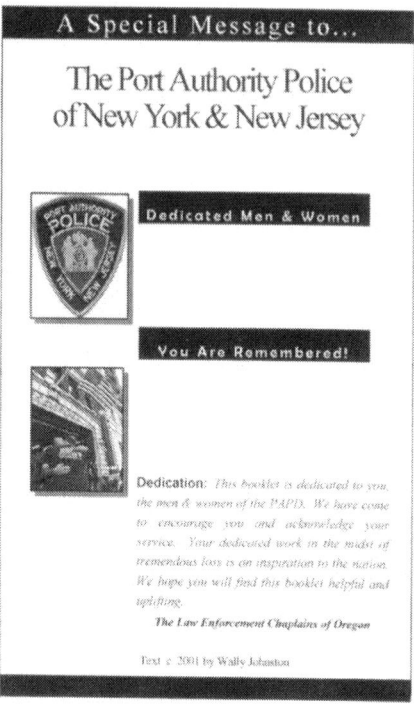

The Port Authority Police, around a 1000 strong, lost 37 officers in the towers. So the impact was huge on that department. The closer it got to the first week of December, 2001, the more I felt the Lord tapping me on the shoulder and encouraging me to go as well. I went. It was the most significant trip of my life!

The author is pictured here holding a poster given to him by the NYPD. In front is a sample of the Bibles we handed out in NYC.
(Photo by Sherwood, OR Gazette Used by permission.)

In New York, chaplains served on-site at Ground Zero, met with personnel in their stations, provided critical incident debriefings, and worked the morgue and shifting of debris and bits of human flesh and bone at Fresh Kills on Staten Island. They attended the seemingly unending funerals of fire fighters and police officers and walked beside the family members. They spent time in the respite rs and offered help through words, a look, a touch, from the Word of God. Thousands of special 9/11 Memorial Bibles were distributed to eager public safety heroes and many found their faith. Unfortunately, the events surrounding 9/11 caused some to question or lose their faith. Regardless of the reactions, their lives will never be the same.

To understand why chaplains responded to such a horrific assignment, we need to understand what motivates them. You will learn, through the window of the 9/11 experience, how public safety chaplains operate and the contributions they make in YOUR city every day.

I've had officers say to me, "Chaplain, I couldn't do your job." I respond to them, "I couldn't do yours." We are all gifted to do certain things. When we combine our gifts, we make a team. Public safety personnel, whether police, fire, or chaplains, usually start out with the same motivation—they want to make a positive difference in their community.

Having pastored for many years, I've had people ask me whether I preferred pastoring or chaplaincy. Without hesitation I tell them chaplaincy. A chaplain is a missionary to a culture we call public safety. They have their own language, walk, and way they conduct their lives. They need someone who is an insider, someone they can trust. That someone is the chaplain. The chaplain and officer will "take a bullet" for each other. Because of their mutual willingness to sacrifice, the public safety officer genuinely appreciates their chaplain and is willing to show it. The people in the pews could learn from them. That sense of teamwork and sacrifice is greater than what is usually found in the church.

Tragedy has a way of bringing out the best or worst in us. Difficulties either bring us closer together or drive us apart. Suffering has true meaning only if it somehow makes us better instead of bitter. September 11, 2001 brought out both reactions. For those of us in public safety, it was a call to duty. That call meant firefighters and police officers ran into burning towers while others ran out. Much like the military, public safety personnel will sacrifice personal safety for their unit.

Among the ranks of such a dedicated and sacrificial group are the men and women who serve as public safety chaplains. They came to New York by the hundreds offering a hand, a heart, and a hug to the many who were still trying to dig out their friends in the rubble of the World Trade Center.

We have this saying, "When the public needs help, they call 9-1-1. When cops or firefighters need help they call their chaplains." Who better to offer assistance at Ground Zero than the chaplains who work with them on a daily basis?

In the coming chapters you will read about the "9/11 Call"—How chaplains understand that their work is a calling from God – a call to service. The "9/11 Heart" will show what is on the inside of chaplains that compels them to serve. The "9/11 Cost" will discuss the sacrifices chaplains make to answer the call to serve; emotionally, economically, spiritually, physically, etc. The "9/11 Reward" shares the benefits the chaplains receive as a result of serving. Finally, "The 9/11 Hope," will discuss the good that has come out of this tragedy and everyday tragedies in local communities, and how we all can benefit from their experiences.

Their stories are the human stories of sacrifice, loss, and hope. You will join in their experiences as you read *Sent to Serve*. You will hear the stories of chaplains who offered their services on 9/11 and for months afterwards.

Many will share a photo but all will share from their hearts. You will also discover:

- How chaplains were utilized
- How the events affected them in the short and long term
- What good has come out of this tragedy
- How their experiences have put into perspective their work as chaplains in local communities

These are the men and women who can help us turn our thoughts from tragedy to hope. As you read, may you come to terms with the events of that day and find hope and healing for your life as well.

Many other chaplains would answer the call to serve in the days, weeks, and months ahead. This is their story. I feel privileged to have been one of those police chaplains who volunteered their time and services in the effort.

Here are some things to remember as you read this book:

- You will see the World Trade Center (WTC) area referred to as "Ground Zero" throughout the book. However, in some quotes you will see it used interchangeably with "Ground Hero." That phrase was often used by the New York public safety and rescue personnel.
- Unless otherwise noted, all scripture quotations are from:

THE HOLY BIBLE, NEW INTERNATIONAL VERSION®, NIV® Copyright © 1973, 1978, 1984, 2011 by Biblica, Inc.™ Used by permission. All rights reserved worldwide.

1 THE 9/11 CALL

"When the call went out for chaplains to assist at Ground Zero, I didn't initially plan on going. But the closer it got to the time for our chaplain group to leave the more I felt God's tap on my shoulder. I was going."

Chaplain Wally Johnston

Little did I realize the impact a smoking tower would have on my future! After I awoke on September 11, 2001, I got the coffee going and turned on the news. I froze in disbelief at what I was seeing. One of the towers of the World Trade Center in New York was on fire! I shook myself and awoke my son as if I needed another human being to verify what I was witnessing. As we stood there, the second tower was hit! This was not an accident — we were under attack!

When we are under attack, God equips men and women in the Body of Christ to overcome evil. The gifts of the Spirit are listed in I Corinthians 12, Romans 12, and Ephesians 4. Among these are five roles or gifts that God gave through the Holy Spirit to guide the churches (some would say these are roles and not formal offices or titles): apostles, prophets, evangelists, pastors, and teachers. In a sense, these roles could be considered a calling. In most cases chaplains are men and women who are called to be pastors (better understood as shepherds). So chaplains are called to be shepherds of the flock (i.e. the police department, military, hospital, fire department, etc.).

Chaplains have been utilized in this country since colonial times. This relationship was first established on April 19, 1775, at the battle of Concord Bridge:

> "A number of New England clerics served at Concord: William Emerson, later to die while on active duty; Joseph Thaxter, soon to be wounded at Bunker Hill; Edmund Foster, a theological student; and the Reverend Doctor Philips Payson. The latter three not only ministered to the minutemen but also 'shouldered their muskets, and fought like common soldiers.' It was written of Rev. Payson: 'Seizing a musket he put himself at the head of a party, and led them forward to the attack.' William Emerson served at Concord in the capacity of a chaplain only, and so has the distinction of being the first Revolutionary War chaplain." [1]

On July 29, 1775, the Continental Congress legally established the military chaplaincy. Military chaplaincy was the forerunner to other chaplaincies, i.e. hospital, police, fire, to name a few. Even though there is a long history, there is still this uncertainty as to what a chaplain is and does. I have found this true within law enforcement circles. Command and personnel don't always know how

---

[1] From the U.S. Army Chaplain Center and School, Fort Jackson, SC, website: www.usachcs.army.mil

to utilize a chaplain. This lack of functional certainty regarding chaplains goes back to before the American Civil War and continues to this day.

When America was attacked on 9/11 many chaplains believed God was calling them to volunteer. They felt God tugging on their hearts to do something. As a chaplain I presented all new officers with a class regarding the chaplaincy service. When I train new officers I tell them that their job is a calling. Romans 13:1-7 discusses the authorities that God places in society to protect us and provide peace. The Living Paraphrase refers to them as "policemen" and Phillips translation as "officers." Some of them may not consider themselves as very spiritual. Regardless, it is a calling and they sense this is where they need to serve the community. Police officers and chaplains have the pull on their hearts to fulfill a much needed role.

In the tenth chapter of St. John we learn about the call of the Shepherd. John paints Jesus as a shepherd, a gate to the sheep fold. Thieves and robbers come into the fold by climbing the fence rather than by walking through the gate. Jesus walks through the gate because the sheep belong to him. He tells them when it is time to leave for their mission: "He calls his own sheep by name and he leads them out. After he has gathered his own flock, he walks ahead of them, and they follow him because they know his voice" (vs. 3 & 4). As God's sheep, all of us can respond to His voice when he calls us to accomplish something.

Chaplains have responded to the call, the voice of the Shepherd, for some time. At the beginning of the American Civil War local pastors felt the call to serve as chaplains.

> "A procession of earnest, sturdy, and buoyant churchmen nevertheless entered into the national

service as chaplains of volunteer regiments. That each one made a great bounding leap of faith is unmistakable. Despite unfavorable portents, each knew in an instant that his place was with the army, and they mustered in at an average of sixty per month from May through December, 1861."[2]

On September 11, 2001 and afterwards, the public safety chaplains from around the country heard the voice of the Shepherd and responded. How were they called to New York? Some were already there like Father Joe D'Angelo, chaplain for the ATF (Alcohol, Tobacco, and Firearms), and the PAPD (Port Authority Police Department of New York and New Jersey).

---

[2] John W. Brinsfield, et. al. , <u>Faith in the Fight, Civil War Chaplains</u> (Mechanicsburg, PA: Stockpole Books, 2008) p. 6. Used by permission.

Father Joe D'Angelo

On September 11, 2001, he was requested to serve the PAPD at the Port Authority Command at JFK International Airport to offer spiritual support and crisis counseling to the officers assigned there. Because he is also an ATF (Bureau of Alcohol, Tobacco, and Firearms) chaplain, he was later that day deployed to their make-shift command in Brooklyn (they had to evacuate their facility at World Trade Center #6 after the attack). Ten days later, Father Joe would visit Ground Zero for the first time, working with the ATF and assisting the police, firefighters, and volunteers who responded from around the nation.

After watching the events unfold on television, Chaplain William Glennie of the U.S. Marshall Service, Arizona Highway Patrol, Sheriff's Office, and FBI called his senators who requested him to go to New York. After speaking with his sergeant at the Arizona Department of Public Safety, they made arrangements with the PAPD for the chaplain to come under their jurisdiction.

Chaplain Jan Heglund was sent by her department, the San Rafael Police Department, CA, to offer assistance at St. Paul's Chapel. This was an Episcopal Church a few blocks away from Ground Zero. Police and fire, iron workers, and volunteers found it an oasis from their difficult tasks. As one officer said to Jan, "It is like home to come in here where it is peaceful and quiet. I come in, and I just don't want to leave."

St. Paul's Chapel

ATF and Waynesboro, Virginia Police chaplain Robert Johnson ended up at the World Trade Center site after assisting in the plane crash of Flight 587 on Long Island. He was there in November and December. During Christmas week he filled in as head of the command center for chaplains, giving the command leader his first 3-day break since the ordeal began. He also visited with Mayor Giuliani during that time.

There were a number of chaplains who were called upon to serve in locations other than Ground Zero. David

Owens, a volunteer chaplain with the Johnson County Sheriff's Office and hospital chaplain, was called upon to respond to the Indianapolis International Airport. He provided comfort and support to travelers, staff, and their families. He even helped conduct worship services in the airport luggage area!

For a majority of the chaplains from around the country, the official call came from the Port Authority Police of New York and New Jersey. The World Trade Center was their jurisdiction. They sent a request to the International Conference of Police Chaplains (ICPC www.icpc4cops.org). This is the largest training and certification organization for police chaplains. They requested those who were certified with the International Critical Incident Stress Foundation (ICISF) to be activated (www.icisf.org). Many chaplains, but not all, are certified with the ICISF to work with individuals and groups to help the first responders normalize their experience and get them back or keep them in service. Critical incident stress is a normal reaction to an abnormal event. I think it's safe to say the 9/11 event was abnormal!

One tool frequently used to cope with Critical Incident Stress (CIS) is a Critical Incident Stress Debriefing (CISD). This is a several stage process to help those in a critical stress incident get back on their feet and continue their work. What aggravated the stress at Ground Zero was the longevity of the event. The attack was quick but the rescue and recovery went on for eight months and 19 days. The recovery went on for months forcing the workers to live the event as it unfolded. That being the case, they could not let their emotional guard down for fear of "losing it" when they were trying to recover their co-workers. This aggravated stress lead many into the clinical condition of Post-Traumatic Stress Disorder or PTSD. We worked with some prime candidates for PTSD when we visited the "Ten House" fire station at Ground Zero (learn more about this in Chapter Two).

Besides those activated by the Port Authority and other agencies, numerous chaplains self-deployed, meaning they came on their own without an invitation. Too many "Lone Rangers" without the accountability of a host group at times made the situation worse. These chaplains were well-intentioned but one result is there will never be a response in this same manner. New guidelines have been put in place to standardize procedures should there be another incident of this magnitude.

On the positive side you have chaplains, like myself, who came as a group with chaplains who had previously served as official on-site chaplains. Our goal was not to work the World Trade Center but to visit, usually by invitation, the precincts and fire stations.

The important thing is that chaplains, like officers, work under authority, not on their own. That is true for all believers. We work under the authority of Jesus Christ. When we work under our own authority we can run into trouble and even do harm. The Apostle Paul was given authority over demons by God. That power was evidenced by the believers in Ephesus for over two years (Acts 19:8-16). There were others who were not under God's authority who were casting out evil spirits. This group... "tried to use the name of the Lord Jesus in their incantations, saying, 'I command you in the name of Jesus, whom Paul preaches, to come out!'" (v.13). Even the evil spirits knew about the authority of Jesus when they replied, "I know Jesus, and I know Paul, but who are you?" (v. 15)

The eighth chapter of Matthew's Gospel describes a Roman Centurion who came to Jesus to seek healing for his servant. Jesus said, "I will come and heal him" (v. 7).

The Centurion (or police officer of that day) told Jesus that he was a man under authority who directed men under his authority. When he gives a command, those under him obey. He told Jesus, "Lord, I am not worthy to have you come into my home. Just say the word from where you are, and my servant will be healed" (v. 8). I make two observations about this story: (1) A man who works under authority is a humble servant and not a tyrant. This man said he was not worthy to have Jesus come into his home; and, (2) he had faith in Jesus' authority. Jesus didn't need to physically be present. He had only to say the word.

There is a chain of command in public safety, especially in law enforcement. All are held accountable within that chain. So the chaplains who were called to serve at Ground Zero needed to work under the umbrella of the proper authority.

A calling is an appointment made by God to direct others in service. Police officers are divinely appointed by God. I remember reading about that in my old green covered Living Bible Paraphrase. At the beginning of Romans 13, it refers to the governing authorities as "policemen." You ought to see the look on officers' faces when I tell them they are called of God!

Remember Father Mulcahy from the "MASH" television series? You've gotta love that guy! His role filled a unique place in that crazy unit. He was part of the troops, yet set apart. He wasn't in a command position but he was considered higher in status than the grunts in the group. Not many attended his services but his services were always needed. That describes the public safety chaplain. I've often said chaplaincy is the best job in the department (by the way, my officers think I'm crazy!). It is a specialty assignment, a niche that only certain people can fill. No one fully understands the chaplain's role but they are quick to utilize him when there is a need. I've tried to explain my work to civilians. Basically, I tell them they don't want me at their front door in the middle of the night. It won't be pretty.

Chaplain Ray Baker is with the Elmore County, Alabama Sheriff's Department and worked with the NYPD Urban Search and Rescue teams at Ground Hero. He says about his call into chaplaincy:

> "As a young pastor, my second funeral was a graveside service for a child who had been killed by her drug addict mother and her boyfriend. I requested that plain clothes and uniformed officers attend the funeral because of the possible danger to the mother who attended in handcuffs. Later the sheriff asked that I consider being on call for his officers. I became the department chaplain."

(Chaplain Baker's assignment in New York was to minister to the New York State Trooper Headquarters Post in the Jacob Jarvis Convention Center.)

Just as God calls or appoints police officers and pastors, he calls chaplains. I remember when God called me to be a chaplain. I was a young associate pastor in Southern California. I had organized a neighborhood watch program and later a Bible study at City Hall. While at the Bible study, an officer came up and asked, "Have you ever considered being a police chaplain?" She gave me a business card with a contact in a neighboring agency. The next thing I knew I was given a tour of the Redondo Police Department and taken out to lunch. They shared about the importance of their program and encouraged me to get involved. Later, I rode with a chaplain from the Los Angeles Police Department. I put together a proposal to start a chaplaincy at our agency and was appointed the first chaplain for the Santa Monica Police Department! When I got home after my first ride along, my wife took one look at me and said, "You've got the bug." Indeed, I had been bitten by God's call. That was 1984 and I still have the "bug."

One day I had my young son riding with me down Wilshire Boulevard in Santa Monica. He said, "Dad, you're a police chaplain right?"

"Yes, son, I am."

"Well how much do police chaplains make?" he inquired.

Finding the question rather interesting I replied, "Chaplains are volunteers."

"Yeah, so how much do they make?"

"Volunteers work but they don't get paid," I explained.

He thought about that for a while and said, "Dad, I think I'm going to be a doctor!"

I came into chaplaincy from a pastoral background. Other chaplains are retired law enforcement officers or firefighters. All have been bitten by the "bug" and enjoy their impossible job.

For Your Consideration

1. Have you ever felt called by God to do something?

2. Consider inviting a local police or fire chaplain to speak to your group about how God moves people into ministry and talk about their call to chaplaincy.

3. What is God calling you to do today?

2 THE 9/11 HEART

"My heart was moved by the great sense of reverence that was displayed by everyone who had responded to assist in the rescue and recovery efforts."

Father Joe D'Angelo – New York Police & Fire Chaplain

Where would you like to have your heart buried? Now that's a strange question! My ancestors fought alongside Sir Robert the Bruce, the King of Scotland, made famous by the movie *Braveheart*.

On his deathbed in 1329, Robert the Bruce asked that his heart be carried into battle against the "Infidels" because he himself had not been able to go on a Crusade. (Apparently organ removal was a common practice in those days.) Bruce's body was buried in Dunfermline Abbey in Scotland and when it was exhumed in 1818 it was found that his ribs had been sawn through, indicating that his heart had indeed been taken from his body.

Sir James Douglas is said to have taken Bruce's heart in a casket with him to Spain in 1330 but, in a battle against the Moors, Douglas was killed. Sir William Keith brought

Bruce's heart back to Scotland and it was buried in Melrose Abbey. There is a plaque on the ground at the place where the heart now lies. The inscription on the stone reads "A noble heart cannot be at peace if freedom is lacking." It incorporates a carving of a heart entwined in the Saltire, the basis of Scotland's national flag. That same heart and Saltire is the focal point of many Johnston coats of arms.

I've never witnessed an open heart surgery. What would you find if you were to perform open heart surgery on the non-physical heart of a chaplain?

What is the most important factor God considers in choosing a king? God sent the prophet Samuel to look for a new king of Israel. He looked over the sons of Jesse. When he saw the tall and strong Eliab he said to himself, "Now's there's the King!" But God told Samuel, "Do not consider his appearance or his height, for I have rejected him. The LORD does not look at the things man looks at. Man looks at the outward appearance, but the LORD looks at the heart" (I Samuel 16:7). With that in mind, David was chosen to be king even though he was the youngest of the group. When God looks for a servant he looks primarily at the heart. When God considers the calling of a chaplain, he looks at the heart as well.

Chaplains come in all shapes and sizes. Guessing from my own experience, we chaplains must be evolving since my shape and size is different from when I started as a chaplain in 1984! Imagine hiring a chaplain on outward appearances alone. "The Look" may be a very important aspect of choosing a Hollywood actor, but it has a minimal role in choosing someone for ministry.

A thesaurus gives such descriptive words to the heart as: *personality, general disposition, central, compassion, response, boldness, bravery, fortitude, nerve, resolution, will, and spirit,* among others. I wrap it all together and refer to heart as *motivation*.

The word comes from the world of psychology which means: "inner or social stimulus for an action".[3] This can also be seen on a spiritual level. What was it that motivated the early Christians to stand by their faith even though it meant death in the Roman arenas? We read in Hebrews Chapter Eleven what people of faith have endured:

> Some faced jeers and flogging, while still others were chained and put in prison.
> [Heb 11:37] They were stoned; they were sawed in two; they were put to death by the sword. They went about in sheepskins and goatskins, destitute, persecuted and mistreated—
> [Heb 11:38] the world was not worthy of them.

When the planes struck the World Trade Center Towers on 9/11/2001, people fled the buildings as best they could. Some, not able to escape, jumped to their deaths. What motivates people like police officers and firefighters to run into such devastation? I have a friend in the NYPD who confides that many New York officers have two or more jobs. I know they don't make enough money to run into buildings to save others. There must be another motivation. As noted in chapter one, officers have a higher spiritual calling, whether they realize it or not.

This same motivation brought hundreds of chaplains to respond at Ground Zero. Their hearts would not let them stay home. Many of them faced all kinds of challenges, physical, financial, etc. John Cundiff, one of the chaplains in our group, had a heart condition. When my friend, Russ Guppy, encouraged him to come, I thought he

---

[3] Online Etymology Dictionary, © 2010 Douglas Harper. Used by permission.

might be pushing his limits. But God protected John during that time and used the earlier experience of tragically losing his wife to help him minister to many. A few years later, John had a heart episode and had to be airlifted to the hospital. We nearly lost him but God spared his life and he continues to serve.

During the week of Christmas, 2001, my friend Chaplain Ken Childress served at Ground Zero. Years earlier, Ken's 15 year old son was killed in an automobile accident while returning home from a church meeting during Christmas week. He happened to be on duty the night his son was killed. He was called to the scene of a fatal accident not knowing until he arrived that his son was the victim. When Ken told me he would be serving at Ground Zero the week of Christmas, I was concerned that he wouldn't be spending Christmas with his family. But Ken needed to come. His special motivation and shared experience with those in New York brought healing to them and himself. In Ken's loss he was able to give to those who lost loved ones in the Twin Towers. The giving brought healing and meaning to his own loss. This, in turn, brought hope to those at Ground Zero who were experiencing loss.

Chaplain Lew Cox from the Des Moines, Washington Police Department knows about tragedy. His daughter was a homicide victim. He could identify with the loss that so many experienced in New York. You'll learn more about Lew in the next few pages.

Heart is also associated with personality. I've heard a lot of talk about the "cop personality" but I wonder if such a thing exists?

This subject was covered in a unique study by Michael Wasilewski & Althea Olson. They begin by asking:

"Does a distinct, recognizable *police personality* exist and, if so, what does it look like? Or might there be a personality profile, that could be determined and tested by existing and accepted measures, into which police officers, and those who aspire to be police officers, fit and can be defined?"

As a chaplain I have found a variety of personalities within the police ranks. They use the elements of their unique personalities to fulfill their role. When officers begin their career, they see the world through the window or prism of their personality. Over time, this worldview changes as they adapt their personalities to their police role. But one must ask, "Which came first, the chicken or the egg?" Do they bring the cop personality package with them or is it developed over time on the job? The consensus is that there is a shift between an officer's pre-employment personality and his or her off-duty personality. So it appears the job does have an effect on an officer's personality. Wasilewski & Olson point out:

"In all the studies conducted to date, there is no definitive police personality profile that has ever been identified, despite the somewhat common belief among many people that one surely exists. Police officers represent a wide variety of personal backgrounds, interests, academic fields of study, hobbies, belief systems, and personalities. How much better if your primary personality, the one you have formed through a lifetime of experience, can meld beneficially with your working personality, so both are tempered and made stronger." [4]

I believe it is good for a department to have diverse personalities much like scripture views the Body of Christ. Each part has its distinct personality and role. Chaplains are no different. Each chaplain's personality makes a contribution to the organization. I served 14 years in a particular department. When I left that department I was happy to recommend my friend, Paul, to fill the vacancy. Paul is a dear brother with a much different personality. I recognized that he would build relationships and have influences in areas that I did not at that department. God is using his unique personality to minister to them today.

I know a lot of chaplains. Their personalities are varied. Some are "Type A" while others are borderline introverts. Central to them all is the desire to serve from a heart of compassion. Like public safety officers, they want to fix what is broken. They like action and they want to make a difference. Some would say they are adrenaline addicts! So when the terrorists struck, they responded by the hundreds from around the country.

Heart is involved in the motivation to serve. For chaplains, this motivation includes:

Compassion:

Chaplains represent the empathetic side of public safety. When officers arrive on a deadly scene they are involved in taking charge and focusing on saving lives and property, not being good listeners to family members. The

---

[4] From "Just a Typical Cop?" by Michael Wasilewski and Althea Olson: April 3, 2011, www.Officer.com. Used by permission.

chaplain stands with the families and focuses on their needs, allowing officers/firefighters to complete their work.

In New York after 9/11, chaplains became that "safe place" for public safety officers to vent their feelings around the event. Since it was the Christmas season, we were asked to meet with the children of police officers and firefighters who lost a parent in the attack on 9/11. They were going to be given some Christmas gifts at the FAO Swartz Toy Store in conjunction with the Marines "Toys-For-Tots" program. We arrived early and noticed a tank and other military equipment around the store. We were escorted to the front of the line and introduced to two athletic young men. They were introduced as "Rangers" so I said, "So, you guys are in the military?" They looked rather puzzled at each other and then said, "No. We are hockey players with the New York Rangers!" Well what do you expect from an old Chicago fan?

We went in first so we could greet the families and mingle among them. I had some copies of my booklet, *A Special Message to the Port Authority Police of New York & New Jersey*, in case I ran into some Port families.

I noticed a couple with kids running around them. The dad wore a Port Authority hat. I introduced myself and gave him a copy of my booklet. When he looked on the back page and saw the names of the fallen officers, he pointed to the name, Bruce Reynolds. He looked at me a little misty-eyed and said, "He was my partner. And this is his wife and their children." My chaplain's heart of compassion went out to them. We visited for some time and the officers said, "Thanks, Chaplain, for being here and giving me this booklet. It means a lot." We were grateful that we were considered "safe places" for officers and their families to vent.

Chaplains also became a liaison to civilian family members who lost loved ones in the attack. Like my friend Ken, Chaplain Lew Cox served at Ground Zero during Christmas (See photo below).

Chaplain Ken Childress (far left) and Lew Cox (third from left)

The following is his account that illustrates the compassion chaplains have while ministering to others. This took place on Christmas day, 2001, at the World Trade Center site:

"When we turned around to leave, to my amazement, there was an older couple standing about fifty feet in front of us. They were very nicely dressed and the lady was holding a bouquet of yellow roses. I was surprised to see these people standing in a restricted area. I asked them who they were and how did they get past the police. They told us that they were George and Charlotte and they had driven down that morning from Connecticut in hopes of placing flowers near the site where their daughter had died on September 11. They said the police officers allowed them to enter Ground Hero to place the flowers.

Their forty-two year old daughter, Jean Marie, was killed when the buildings collapsed. I asked them if they would like me to pray with them before they placed the flowers. They said, yes, so Bill and I accompanied them to the edge of the pit of Ground Hero. The heat from the sun had a pleasant feeling and there was an awareness that something special was about to take place.

We went before the Lord where the World Trade Center buildings once stood. We committed Jean Marie into the Lord's hands and gave tribute to her short life. We repeated the "Lord's Prayer" together. Officer Pollock stood behind us with his head bowed in reverence. I looked over at him and I saw tears running down his face as we memorialized Jean Marie's life. I could also sense a strong presence of the Holy Spirit in our midst. After we prayed, Jean Marie's parents placed the yellow roses up against a concrete barrier at the edge of the pit of the World Trade Center. With tears in our eyes we stepped back for a moment of silence.

On that dreadful day their daughter had an early morning meeting at the World Trade Center. She worked for a company that was located a few blocks from the Center. She was the only employee from her company at the Trade Center that day. She was engaged to be married. The wedding was scheduled for March of 2002, and she had already bought her wedding dress. An added sad note about Jean Marie's death, her father worked as an engineer on the construction of the World Trade Center project.

I told these folks that I was on common ground with them and their grief. I explained to them I experienced having a daughter murdered, too. Of course, there was an instant bond between us. We realized we were a part of the same club. I told them it was an honor and a privilege to have been able to pray with them and to be able to pay tribute to their daughter's life."

Conviction: *'a fixed or firm belief '.*

People need a message from the heart of God. That doesn't mean chaplains should come in preaching. As a matter of fact, that is the last thing they should do. Theirs is a ministry by *permission.* Chaplains should not have a spiritual agenda. They should leave that up to the Lord. Chaplains, however, should respond with conviction when spiritual questions are being asked of them.

After a few months on my first chaplain assignment, my wife was visiting the police department with me. One of the officers came up to her and said, "We didn't know what to expect when your husband came on board. We thought he might come in Bible thumping, but he didn't. He's just a good resource and friend."

The foundations of many officers were shaken after 9/11. They needed someone who would be a person of conviction who could show them a foundational belief that would sustain them.

The 84th Precinct in New York is just across the street from Metro Tech, which houses the 9-1-1 center in Brooklyn. The officers from that precinct provided security for Metro Tech. We had been invited there to meet the officers. We presented them with special edition 9/11 Memorial Bibles (See photo below).

At the 84th Precinct in Brooklyn, NY: Chaplain Russ Guppy (far left), his son John (far right). Chaplain John Cundiff, kneeling and Chaplain Wally Johnston standing to his left.

A sample of the Bibles we handed out in New York City.

God's Word for Peace Officers contains an introduction with a number of tools that directs readers to certain portions of scripture that addresses a need. As a sergeant took her Bible, she asked, "Where can I find answers to my questions about faith?" I directed her to the helps section in the back of the Bible. As we pulled away from the station, I noticed her sitting outside the building, head down, looking at her Bible. I have prayed numerous times that the Holy Spirit would use that Bible to assist her in finding that foundation for her life. Chaplains are persons of conviction delivering a message of hope.

Empathy:

Chaplains need to identify with the pain of others without making it their own and ending up burned-out or experiencing compassion fatigue. Burnout is when one is so overwhelmed that they shut down and don't care anymore. Compassion fatigue is like a person trying to spin several plates on the end of sticks. They are caring too much and feel overwhelmed. Eventually something gets dropped or broken.

When one acts out of empathy, one identifies with the situation of another. This needs to be coupled with healthy boundaries that prevent one from codependency, burnout, or compassion fatigue. Boundaries are those invisible lines that distinguish one person from another. When families are enmeshed, they have poor boundaries. Codependency is when someone lives or grew up in an addictive home. Codependents enable, quite often unknowingly, the addict to continue in their addiction. They are the family caretakers, the ones who make the family look good.

Healthy, genuine empathy is an element that chaplains bring to the table of tragedy, making those who suffer grief feel that they are not alone. Another human being cares and has some understanding.

Authenticity:

Authenticity has to do with being genuine and involves ministering without an agenda. God has to work on our hearts in a process to make us real. Remember the classic children's story "The Velveteen Rabbit"? The rabbit knew there was something different about the Skin Horse. The other toys represented something that was real—like a model boat was a representation of a "real" boat. (But they weren't real themselves). One day the rabbit asked the old skin horse, who had outlived all of the other fad toys, "What is REAL?" They carry on a discussion for a while and then the rabbit asks if becoming real happens all at once. The Skin Horse tells him it takes a long time and involves some personal costs of wear and tear. That is the cost of becoming "real."

Authentic 'servanthood' means giving of one's self without looking for payback. Chaplains were not the only authentic servants who served after 9/11. In October, 2001, actress Brooke Shields, among others, paid a visit to the Marriott Hotel across the street from Ground Zero. The Marriott opened its doors to emergency personnel for a number of months following the attack. It became a place for them to eat and get some rest. Ms. Shields came that night to work the serving line for the men and women of New York's Bravest and Finest and others from different parts of the country.

Nino's restaurant was located just blocks from the World Trade Center. Authentic servant volunteers from around the nation were there to serve meals to public safety officers. As in most places where emergency workers gather, children sent notes and drawings that literally covered the walls from top to bottom.

This drawing displays chaplains at the WTC:

The restaurant remained open for months to provide meals and a respite for the workers.

Nino's volunteers served us meals.

According to Chaplain Lew Cox:

"Nino's is a family restaurant that is about three blocks from Ground Zero. The family shut the restaurant down permanently to feed only those working at Ground Zero. It is fashioned like St. Paul's Church. It has thousands of messages, flags, drawings, pictures, cards and letters. All the food is donated with volunteer cooks. Nino's is an experience, and I'm glad my last meal at Ground Hero was at Nino's. When the World Trade Center is cleaned up, Nino's Restaurant will be taken to the Smithsonian Institute."

Actually, the restaurant will not be there, but a sample apron from Nino's with police and fire patches is.

These authentic volunteers helped everywhere. One student carried extra copies of the Memorial Edition of

God's Word For Peace Officers. During his break serving at St. Joseph's Chapel across the street from Ground Zero, he would hand them out wherever he saw officers in the city. A German film crew interviewed him at St. Joseph's and got a close-up of the Bible cover. They told him that Bible would be seen throughout Germany on television that night!

The process of becoming a chaplain who is "real" can have its trials and desert places, but officers need to see how chaplains work through their own personal 9/11's. It takes time and relationship building to earn the trust of those we serve.

Healthy Transparency:

The chaplain learns to appropriately self-disclose their own inner struggles. Police officers are not usually good about opening up or letting out their emotions. As chaplains we can model healthy ways to self-disclose. Chaplains need to inform them of the unhealthy outcome of not opening up.

To illustrate this, there is an old church camp game called "Chubby Bunny." I'm sure it's known by other names but the effect is the same. Rows of unwitting volunteers sit in chairs in front of the crowd. A team member stands behind them. At the signal, the team member places a marshmallow in the mouth of his partner. After each marshmallow, they have to say "Chubby Bunny." This continues until there is only one person left with puffy cheeks that can say "Chubby Bunny." For a while it's easy to say it, but as time goes on and the mouth gets full, it becomes difficult. One gets to the point of either swallowing or spitting out the marshmallows. Now that I'm older and wiser, I wouldn't suggest participating in this game. I heard someone ended up choking to death. Not a good thing.

Our emotions are like the marshmallows. We can stuff them. Early on we have the ability to express them if we choose. But if we keep stuffing, we lose our ability to express what is going on inside. This leads to depression (stuffing) or anger (spitting the mess out).

Unfortunately for the Ground Zero workers, especially the firefighters, they didn't want to open up. They were afraid if they opened up the dam would break and they would "lose it." They felt they had to keep it together to face their daily task of searching for their fellow firefighters. We paid a visit to the Ten House Fire Station at the World Trade Center site. They were very guarded and we didn't know if they would let us in. We knocked several times and finally the door opened a crack and a voice said, "What do you want?"

"We are chaplains from the west coast. We came by to offer our support and to give you this poster from a fire chief in Oregon." Shortly after that, the door opened. It took several minutes for the crew to warm up to us. After they felt more comfortable they began to open up.

A firefighter asked, "Would you like to go on the roof?" The roof of the Ten House Fire Station was sacred ground. The entire shift lost their lives on September 11, 2001. The roof had a panoramic view of the "pit"—what they called the huge crater of World Trade Center rubble. Our host excused himself and left us to view the devastation. I remember calling my wife from that roof and seeing papers floating out of nearby offices. Our host was lifting weights in a room on the roof. For the next two hours he would work for a time and then come out to speak to us about 9/11 until he got misty-eyed. He would then go back to his workout until his return trip. They were trying to keep it in but I was so glad God placed us there for them. When we left, our firefighter host gave each of us a hug and thanked us for coming.

Front of the Ten House Fire Station @ Ground Hero

Engine leaves the Ten House (Photos taken by author, 2009)

Humility:

There is no room for narcissism. A chaplain is a team player that puts the team above selfish needs. If you know how humble you are, then you probably aren't! If a chaplain gets big on himself, then there is no room for those he serves.

Humility is illustrated in the comparison of the prayers of the Pharisee and the tax collector in Luke 18:10-14:

> "Two men went up to the temple to pray, one a Pharisee and the other a tax collector.
>
> The Pharisee stood up and prayed about himself: 'God, I thank you that I am not like other men—robbers, evildoers, adulterers—or even like this tax collector.
>
> I fast twice a week and give a tenth of all I get.'
>
> "But the tax collector stood at a distance. He would not even look up to heaven, but beat his breast and said, 'God, have mercy on me, a sinner.'
>
> "I tell you that this man, rather than the other, went home justified before God. For everyone who exalts himself will be humbled, and he who humbles himself will be exalted."

An effective chaplain promotes others above himself. I feel rather uncomfortable around someone who continually talks about themselves. There is an element of self-promotion that is healthy and needed. It becomes a problem when self-promotion comes before others. If we are doing our job, those we serve will be our promoters. It looks better coming from them and is more effective!

Honesty:

Lack of honesty will destroy an officer/firefighter's, or chaplain's career. I have heard of chaplains who may have been well intentioned who told a little fib in order to avoid disclosing confidential information rather than simply refusing to disclose. The end result was their dismissal over the lie. Most officers endure at least one internal affairs investigation during their career. They mess up on the job or a citizen complains. Most often they are cleared or reprimanded but there are those occasional firings. In those cases, it often involves the officer's lying about something during the investigation. The most common thing that ends a pastor's career is an affair. For officers or chaplains, it's a lie.

An honest, healthy good sense of self:

The Greek philosopher Socrates (469 - 399 B.C.) said, "Know thyself." That sounds simple, but for most it is a life journey. Public safety chaplains are ordinary people with out-of-the-ordinary jobs. Like anyone else, they are on a journey of self-discovery.

One of the building blocks of self-esteem is praise. I was asked, "What is one of the rewards of being a chaplain?" My response, "The genuine praise and appreciation I receive from those I serve." While serving in New York City, chaplains were treated with awe, respect, and genuine appreciation. We were given access to most places. This made it handy while driving in the city. We were there when Mayor Giuliani lit the Christmas tree at Ground Zero. We arrived early. We asked the officer at the intersection if we could park at a certain place.

Apologetically, he replied, "Fellas, normally I would let you park anywhere but the Mayor is only a few minutes away and we need that space. Would you mind parking back there?" Though we did not know it before we arrived in NYC, the praise and admiration we received was a growing motivation during our service there.

Some chaplains grew up in addictive homes and learned to take on roles in order to survive. Some became family "heroes" who kept everything together and made the family look good to the outside world. This developed into codependency. Because of this, chaplains must avoid taking on the "stuff" that belongs to officers or citizens. They need to set appropriate boundaries. A personal boundary is like a coffee filter, keeping out the grounds but allowing the flavor and water through. At times, people try to give us their "coffee grounds" of issues they have created and must claim for themselves. Chaplains should be aware of this, especially if they grew up in a dysfunctional family system. Codependents run from their own personal pain by taking care of others. Like one codependent said, "I dreamed I died and saw everybody else's life pass before my eyes!"

Chaplains need to know themselves well enough to realize if they have a healthy or unhealthy care for others. They must not run from their pain to fix the pain of others. At the heart of an effective chaplain is a self-esteem that is balanced and whole.

When the terrorists hit on 9/11, a command post was set up. This was the center, the heart of the operation. It's all part of the Incident Command System (ICS). It provides structure, defines responsibilities, and devises a chain of command for an incident. The command center of any critical operation must be protected or the mission can be compromised. This system was refined and then required following the events of 2001. Now, any responders to an incident must be certified in ICS (Incident Command System) through the Department of Homeland Security to participate.

The heart is the command center for chaplains. It provides the passion and drive that keeps a chaplain engaged. It is important to keep the command center away from danger and never let it be compromised. Philippians 4:7 reminds us…His peace "will guard your hearts and minds in Christ Jesus." Jesus also said, "Peace I leave with you; my peace I give to you…do not let your hearts be troubled and do not be afraid" (John 14:27).

For Your Consideration

1. Find out about your local chaplain program. Invite them to your church to share their heart with the congregation.

2. Many agencies conduct Citizen's Academies. The academy teaches citizens about the different aspects of their local department and how they can get involved. Quite often a chaplain will be an instructor in these academies. It would be a great opportunity for you to connect with your local chaplain and agency. You may find opportunities to volunteer.

3. What did you learn about your heart as you read this chapter? What qualities do you have that can be used by God to meet the needs of others?

3 THE 9/11 COST

"I am not able to tell anyone what is going on here and have them understand the magnitude of the pain that is in this city. It is something that has to be seen, smelled, and heard. The heartbreak is heavy in the air."

Chaplain Beth Wilson – Spokane, WA Police Department

My wife and I had just ordered our meal at the restaurant to celebrate our wedding anniversary when I was dispatched to a tough call. I had to leave her there (my son brought her home). In this line of business you never know when you will be called upon to help someone in crisis. It is the cost to one's schedule and the cost of serving.

We can only begin to estimate the cost for the public safety officers at Ground Zero. Chaplain Beth Wilson describes some of the personal costs:

"These men and women are exhausted. They are working 12 hours a day for six days and then take one day off. On their day off they are trying to be there for their families and getting all the other errands done. They don't have any down time let alone any time to catch up on their sleep. I did help one officer look at his calendar far enough ahead to take his day off before Christmas to get a tree and decorate it. He will be working every holiday and he says that hurts. Another officer has two small children and his wife is pregnant with number three. He says that she has been real sick and doesn't want to complain or make him worry. He said all he can do for her right now is to hire a housekeeper. He said he would trade all his overtime to be home more with his family."

I asked chaplains on a survey what it cost them to serve at Ground Zero. Many said their financial costs were met by their ministry or community. Most of the cost couldn't be figured on a calculator because it couldn't be seen. There are those hidden costs of ministry of which many people are unaware unless they are engaged in ministry. Those costs are probably why pastors write out a resignation on Mondays! I know I have, only to tear it up until the next week.

Jesus reminds us in Luke 14:25-33 that there is a cost to following him in ministry. Our love for him should be greater than anything else: parents, family, even our own life. A chaplain, like an officer, knows that he may one day have to take a bullet for another officer. I've often said that cops are more tightly knit than most church folks in that they would take a bullet for someone else. Would the person in the pew next to you at church do the same?

Many clergy have given up lucrative careers to follow the call to serve. I conducted a seminar for some pastors. I went to lunch with a couple of the younger men. Jason told me he had been an electrical engineer before he got involved in youth ministry. He gave up a six figure salary and basically took a vow of poverty to go into professional ministry. He harbors no regrets. He believes he is following the call of God and is fulfilled in his service in the Kingdom. Most professional clergy probably feel the same as Jason.

When you think about it, there is a cost for most people to follow their passion—years of training and education, long hours, uncertain finances. Yet, the goal we pursue makes the sacrifice bearable. Paul said, "I run for the heavenly prize" (see Philippians 3:12-14). One doesn't win the prize without discipline, sacrifice, or finishing the race.

There was a cost for chaplains to respond to Ground Zero:

Financial

Chaplain Steve Lee put the cost of thousands of Bibles on his personal credit card to get the Word out to first responders at Ground Zero. There is no way to put a price tag on the value of God's Word at such a time. Lives were touched and transformed (Please see photo on next page).

Chaplain Steve Lee of Peace Officer Ministries (POM)

One example of this transformation took place at the Metro Tech E-911 Center in Brooklyn (See photos page 51). I wanted to be sure we visited with dispatchers. They are the faceless heroes of 9/11. They heard their officers call for help as the Twin Towers came down. They felt helpless as they heard the destruction over the airwaves. On September 11, 2001 they took 55,574 calls for service that resulted in the dispatch of 12,600 radio calls to units in the field! We had stopped by on a Saturday to visit at the center and gave out a few cases of the Bibles. When we handed out the last of the Bibles and were leaving, we heard footsteps behind us. Dispatchers were running after us and said, "We didn't get one of those Bibles. Will you bring us some?" We promised we would be back. Later, one of the supervisor sergeants called and asked, "Can you can get us more Bibles?" We asked him how many dispatchers they had and he said 1,300! We explained that we had only a rental car and would not be able to bring a large quantity with us. The sergeant said, "No problem. I'll have one of our officers meet you with a marked NYPD van to load them up." So on Monday, we met at the Billy Graham Center on W. 25th Street and loaded a ton of Bibles. Our first stop was One Police Plaza, the NYPD headquarters. We wanted to be sure the families of the fallen twenty-three officers received a copy. Then it was on to Metro Tech.

As we pulled up to the dispatch building, officers with hand trucks unloaded the cases of Bibles and began stacking them in a room. We had a few copies out and were signing the presentation page for some of the dispatchers. We thought we would simply be handing out a few Bibles but as I looked down the hall, people were lined up the full length of the building! Before we knew it, the Sergeant had a table set up for us with bottled water. It looked like a book signing at a major bookstore. As we signed over the copies of "God's Word for Peace Officers," we made it a point to thank each dispatcher for their dedicated service and thanked them for their work on that fateful day. At one point I heard my friend Russ speaking. I looked and he was praying with one of the dispatchers! This went on for nearly three hours.

This was made possible because someone like Chaplain Steve Lee took the financial risk of putting the order for thousands of Bibles on his personal credit card.

SENT TO SERVE...THE CHAPLAINS OF 9/11

Shift change at Metro Tech 911 Center in Brooklyn, NY. Dispatchers and officers wanted the chaplains to sign their Bibles.

So many came to receive Bibles they set up a table to accommodate the crowd. (Chaplain Wally Johnston in front, John Cundiff in middle, and Russ Guppy on the end. This became a two to three hour event.

Chaplain Guppy added:

> "Over and over again we heard from the communications staff, 'Thank you for remembering us!' They thanked us because in the nearly three months since 9/11, they had received no specific intervention, care, or time off to deal with the enormous stress and trauma they endured during and following the attack on the twin towers."

For the most part, people don't realize that the vast majority of police chaplains in America are volunteers. They are pastors whose churches allow them to take time to serve in their capacity as chaplains. They give their time and money to drive their cars, take officers out to coffee or meals, entertain, and buy equipment and clothing among other ways to serve. It would be interesting if one could calculate the dollars saved in departments by the free services their chaplains provide. It would probably go a long way to ending our national debt! You are not going to hear any of this from chaplains. They don't ask for things for themselves. I guess chaplains haven't learned the verse that says, *"Ask and it will be given to you; seek and you will find; knock and the door will be opened to you.* (Matthew 7:7-8). It becomes too awkward for a chaplain to ask so they need an advocate in their department. This is someone who is fully committed to the ministry of chaplaincy and will go to bat for him/her. I had such an advocate in the departments in which I served. One captain took a look at me and said, "Do you need anything? I think you should have a patrol jacket. Wally, head down to supply to get one." He also made sure I had a dress uniform so I would look sharp at public services.

The chaplain's attire has always been an issue in the military or law enforcement. That's because the role of the chaplain has always been misunderstood, mysterious, or unknown. The chaplains of the Civil War had a tough time getting outfitted due to lack of clear guidelines and full acceptance of their official duties from the men they served. A colonel in a New York regiment told his chaplain: "You are to be pastor of the regiment, and your uniform should be what would be suitable for a minister of the gospel." Other officers felt the chaplain should be in full uniform, all the way down to the sabre! It depended greatly on the unit commander and today's police chaplain's attire is dependent upon the opinion of the chief and command staff.

This lack of uniformity in police dress was evident in my career, having served four agencies. The first and second agencies issued me only a photo ID. The third issued me patrol and dress uniforms, a badge, and a photo ID. The last agency had me serve as chaplain for the city as well as the department and issued a dress uniform, a photo ID, and a badge.

Chaplains need advocates in their communities who will let their departments and cities know what they need. Individuals, churches, and groups can inform their police departments that they want to help provide for the chaplains (see "For Your Consideration" at the end of the chapter).

It is obvious that many don't realize that police chaplaincy is not a career on which to build a financial future. I was annually asked to take a couple of college students with me on Professional Development Day. Students would inform the school what careers they were interested in and be matched with a professional in the field. I was amazed to learn that these young people would consider a career in public safety chaplaincy. One of the first things I taught them is that this is not a career that has great financial benefits. I proceeded to tell them that most chaplains are volunteers and the few who are paid are usually part time. It takes years to get to the place where chaplaincy becomes a paid assignment.

In many ways the chaplain doesn't receive much remuneration because most of his work is unseen. It is one-on-one and confidential. You won't glean much about the chaplain's work from the departmental newsletter. Because of this, when departmental budgets run short, it is the funding for the chaplain that often gets cut.

Away from family

While we were with family celebrating Christmas in 2001, there was a team of chaplains who were away from their homes serving at Ground Zero (refer to photo in Chapter Two).

Whenever an officer dies, it has a great impact on a department. I've conducted a couple of police funerals. From the time the officer died to the time of the service, I was going non-stop for over two weeks. There were so many details needing attention. My troops needed me, their families needed me, family came in from around the country who needed escorting, the service had to be planned, and on and on. I would come home at the end of each day and just fall in bed. I didn't have the time or energy to be present for my own family. I don't remember my dear wife complaining during those times but she had every right to complain. She was willing to postpone her desire to be with me. I guess that is why at my retirement party our department presented Linda with flowers and thanked her for sharing me with them.

Emotional

The traumatic incidents with which chaplains work can have an emotional toll on them. People often say to me, "You chaplains help others deal with the emotional baggage but who takes care of you, Chaplain?" That's a good question. Chaplains have a built in support system. Many spouses help with this but they must be careful not to get traumatized themselves (secondary trauma). Chaplains also have other chaplains. I've been fortunate to work with a great group of chaplains in our area. We meet monthly to "debrief" each other.

Chaplains, like all people, need healthy personal boundaries. Otherwise, they take on too much of others' personal stuff and after a while the burden gets too heavy. A personal boundary is that which distinguishes us from another person and his issues. After all, we have our own issues! But others want to give us theirs! When someone shares something with us and we need to own it, that's healthy. But what if we don't need to own it? A healthy boundary will leave it with that person so it doesn't infect us. After my mother died, all of the stuff that belonged to others made my life toxic. The father of one of our church members died. I was with the family in the hospital when the word came about his death. We gathered in a circle for prayer and I told them, "I feel your pain." That was not a figure of speech; I really felt their pain mixed in with my own complicated grief. It was okay to feel empathy for them, but I was adding their grief on top of mine and it was killing me!

The "boundary burden" we can carry is illustrated in the movie "The Mission" starring Robert De Niro. It's about 18th century Spanish Jesuits who try to protect a remote South American Indian tribe in danger of falling under the rule of pro-slavery Portugal. De Niro, in the part of Mendoza, is one of the slave hardened traders. He ends up killing his brother for having an affair with his fiancé. He falls into a depression and repents, to become a Jesuit priest. For his self-imposed penance, he carries heavy armor and equipment up a steep mountain trail with the Indians and priests. The burden gets overwhelming. Father Gabriel takes his knife and cuts the net holding the burden and it tumbles down the cliff. Mendoza breaks into tears, relieved of his burden and depression.

Police officers, and even some chaplains, use dark humor to deal with the traumas they face (also called black humor, cop humor, etc.). Cops will say anything during and after a traumatic incident just to get through it. To the civilian ear it sounds inappropriate. This humor is not unlike what one might hear behind the scenes in an emergency room, or from firefighters, EMT's, and dispatchers. In the wrong setting it is inappropriate but not among emergency workers. As an example (please don't be offended), one Halloween I went to our dispatch center dressed in a British Bobbie hat, big nose, mustache, dark rimmed glasses, with a stogie. I walked up to this dispatcher who was dressed in a nun outfit. I said in a disguised voice, "Who are you?" She replied, "I'm a &%$# pregnant nun. Who in the &%$# are you!" So I lifted my disguise and said, "The chaplain." You should have seen the shocked look on her face as she volunteered some additional creative adjectives!

Ground Zero was not an isolated event. It went on for many months so the workers, especially the firefighters, felt they couldn't talk about it for fear of "losing it."

Many chaplains experienced nightmares, sleep problems, and other symptoms after serving on site. I had some dreams about Ground Zero for a time after I returned to "normal" life.

For some, their time at Ground Zero had a healing effect on their emotions. It provided an outlet for their personal grief to care for those who lost loved ones at the World Trade Center. 9/11 was an emotional mixed bag. Tragically, there were suicides within the public safety family after 9/11.

Political

Ministry should never have to be political but guess what? There is politics in education, in business and even in the church. It is probably the one area that can cause the greatest obstacles for a chaplain. By politics I'm not referring to Republican, Democrat, Independent, etc. Jesus had to deal with politics among the disciples. There was that time when the disciples James and John sought favors with Jesus:

> [35] Then James and John, the sons of Zebedee, came to him. "Teacher," they said, "we want you to do for us whatever we ask."
>
> [36] "What do you want me to do for you?" he asked.
>
> [37] They replied, "Let one of us sit at your right and the other at your left in your glory."
>
> [38] "You don't know what you are asking," Jesus said. "Can you drink the cup I drink or be baptized with the baptism I am baptized with?"
>
> [39] "We can," they answered.
>
> Jesus said to them, "You will drink the cup I drink and be baptized with the baptism I am baptized with, [40] but to sit at my right or left is not for me to

grant. These places belong to those for whom they have been prepared."

⁴¹ When the ten heard about this, they became indignant with James and John. ⁴² Jesus called them together and said, "You know that those who are regarded as rulers of the Gentiles lord it over them, and their high officials exercise authority over them. ⁴³ Not so with you. Instead, whoever wants to become great among you must be your servant ⁴⁴ and whoever wants to be first must be slave of all. ⁴⁵ For even the Son of Man did not come to be served, but to serve, and to give his life as a ransom for many" (Mark 10).

There is dysfunctional leadership in departments as in families. Being a chief in a police department can be ego building. I have heard of chiefs who actually developed a narcissistic personality disorder. Chaplains not only have to deal with the dysfunctions in their departments but must also help others deal with that dysfunction.[5] Keep in mind the vast majority of chiefs are good leaders. There is a difference between a leader and a manager. The difference is that leaders inspire those they lead and command respect; managers force their will on others and demand respect. Happy is a chaplain who serves a leader.

Health

Some chaplains developed what was called the "Ground Zero Cough" after breathing in the airborne substances at the World Trade Center. Alfred Thompson was a 76 year old chaplain for the FDNY when the

---

[5] For further reading I recommend <u>Overcoming the Dark Side of Leadership</u> by Gary L. McIntosh & Samuel D. Rima, Sr., Baker Book House, 2007.

terrorists attacked the World Trade Center. The Methodist minister was at home on Long Island and drove to Manhattan just in time to see the first tower collapse. After about six weeks working at Ground Zero, he was hospitalized for bronchitis and pneumonia. He is now 85 and lives with his son in Massachusetts, still battling the health effects of his service.

On Sunday, January 2, 2011, President Obama signed into law the James Zadroga 9/11 Health and Compensation Act. The bill covers first responders, volunteers, morgue workers and those who lived or went to school near Ground Zero. Detective Zadroga died on January 6, 2006, as a result of respiratory disease, black lung disease, and mercury on the brain. His death was directly linked to his work at Ground Zero.

For Your Consideration

1. Each October is designated "Clergy Appreciation Month." Most people generally see this as "Pastor Appreciation Month." But clergy serve in various roles, including chaplaincy. Contact your denominational headquarters and encourage them to recognize chaplains in October. Also, contact the leadership in your local church with the same appeal. Perhaps you could volunteer to head a committee to see that pastors and chaplains get recognized. If you are not sure there are public safety chaplains in your community, contact your local police and fire department and find out. You could invite the chaplain to a recognition service at your church.

2. Chaplains need advocates in their communities. Find out how you can support your local chaplains.

4 THE 9/11 REWARD

*"So many came with tears, hugged me and expressed their thanks for coming to help them.
Many said that without us chaplains they could not have made it through the pain."*

Chaplain James Cox, Wythe County Virginia Sheriff's Office

I was once asked, "What is the most rewarding thing for you as a chaplain?" You will understand when I tell you about Officer Chad. Chad was a motorcycle cop. We call them motor cops. One Sunday after church I received a phone call from Chad.

"Hey Wally, can we get together to talk?"

"Sure, Chad," I replied, "When would you like to do that?"

With a somewhat desperate sound in his voice he said, "How about now?"

So we agreed to meet in a vacant lot in Los Angeles. We walked around for two hours as I listened to Chad unload his fears, shame, and lack of purpose. Chad was trying to find and save his life. In fact each year there are three to four times as many officers who kill themselves than those killed on duty. Chad asked me to help him out of the spiritual darkness he was in. So I shared Jesus' life with Chad. Before we left that parking lot, he received Jesus Christ into his life. We followed up together with some discipleship training.

One day I was driving through the parking lot of the police department when Chad flagged me down.

"Tell me it isn't true. I heard you are moving away."

"Yes indeed I am. We are moving back to the Midwest."

"If it weren't for you, I wouldn't have my job!"

That is the chaplain's reward. I have a number of plaques presented to me over the years but the chaplain's reward is reflected on the back of my departmental trading card:

> "The chaplain finds it rewarding to know that he has helped an officer during a time of personal trauma, affording the officer the opportunity to get back on his or her feet and continue their service to the community."

There is a different level of commitment among public safety personnel. I pastored for a number of years and, for the most part, I loved the parishioners and they loved me. However, of all my church assignments, I don't think any of those folks would take a bullet for me. I could be wrong but eating lead for their pastor isn't what they saw as "taking up their cross daily." Yet there is no doubt in my mind that officers would take a bullet for me as I would for them. Matters of life and death bring relationships to a new level. It's not unlike officers who train together in the academy. They get close there. Once they are on the job at their department and are called to a situation requiring them to give their life for the other, the relationship changes. They are enjoying a new level of commitment.

I once went on a call-out with our SWAT team to an incident involving an armed and barricaded suspect. Just before the team deployed, the eyes of my camouflaged sergeant met mine. Nothing had to be said. We were there for each other. The reward was in the relationship. That's why so many military types would rather serve another tour of duty…they get tight with their unit. They are there for each other.

I see the reward in the faces of those I serve. When we made our first visit to Ground Zero, we went to the Ten House Fire Station. This was the firehouse located just across the street from the WTC. I had produced a booklet called *A Special Message to the Port Authority Police of New York and New Jersey*. It was a message to encourage them and remember their fallen. The back cover was a tribute listing each of the 37 fallen Port officers who died in the tower. Upstairs in the firehouse, I saw a young Port Authority officer sitting next to a table, leaning back on his chair, with a distant stare. I knelt beside him to show him the booklet. We came to the back cover. There he saw the name of a friend he went to the academy with. He said, "Thanks Chaplain. I really appreciate this booklet." That's the reward.

Here are some responses from other chaplains at Ground Zero regarding their reward of serving there:

William Glennie is a chaplain with the sheriff's officer, U.S. Marshall Services, Arizona Highway Patrol, and the FBI: The reward at Ground Zero was…"witnessing how God met the people in their grief and loss." Through the years he has also seen a number of officers come to faith in Christ. Part of the reward is being asked to perform a spiritual role. When Bill reported for duty each day, the public safety officers would say with heavy Irish-New York accents, "Good mornin' Fadda. Are you going to bless me today?" He would stop and pray before they began work.

Bill went on to say:

"One night I was debriefing a fire captain and on completion I mentioned that I would pray for him each day. He looked at me with that 'I've heard that before' look. He then said,

'Let me sign your hard hat to remind you.'

'Okay,' I said.

When others saw his name they asked to sign my hat as well. It is covered with their names and numbers and I pray each day for them."

Many plaques, awards, or trophies end up on a wall or shelf. Some may be packed away in storage. The "trophies" for chaplains are explained in the poem on the next page:

LIVING TROPHIES
by Wally Johnston
Dedicated to Law Enforcement Chaplains
© 2003

You cannot lose a trophy
That's made of special things
Of material so precious
That cannot be found in rings.
For the trophies that I speak of
Are not placed upon a shelf
To take up space and gather dust
Or to focus on oneself.
Living trophies are what make a man
Feel blessed beyond all measure
Investing in another's life
Is valued more than treasure.
A chaplain's trophies move about
In uniforms of blue
That serve the public everyday
Including me and you.
His walls remain uncluttered
But his life is all-complete
Because one day he'll have so much
To lay at Jesus' feet.
Thank you Chaplains for helping us
To know what really counts
That people are the things to build
Not trophies and their mounts
It takes a special person
One that knows the art of giving
To remind us legacies are built
With trophies that are living.

The officers walking the halls, riding a cruiser, working at Ground Zero…those are a chaplain's trophies.

5 THE 9/11 HOPE

"...to comfort those who mourn, and provide for those who grieve in Zion—to bestow on them a crown of beauty instead of ashes, the oil of gladness instead of mourning, and a garment of praise instead of a spirit of despair."
(Isaiah 61:3)

We tend to look for meaning in tragedy, yet the writer of Ecclesiastes pens, *"Meaningless! Meaningless!" says the Teacher. "Utterly meaningless! Everything is meaningless"* (Ecclesiastes 1:2). The writer is saying that, apart from God, nothing has meaning, nothing makes sense. Some became overwhelmed in their loss after 9/11 and turned to bitterness. None of it made sense to them. I believe there may be no meaning in tragedy itself. The meaning comes about in our cooperation with God's purposes through that tragedy. God didn't bring the Twin Towers down as some "Christian" extremists declared. But when we turn to Him in the midst of the rubble, He brings meaning to our response. Meaning comes in our turning to Him! Part of what brought meaning to 9/11 was the spiritual response of turning to God.

God can bring good out of evil. The story of Joseph is a great example of the evil intentions of men and how God can work through those to bring about His glory. As you recall, Joseph was sold into slavery by his brothers who later came to Egypt to purchase grain. The crowning verse of that story is in chapter fifty of Genesis, verse 20: *"You intended to harm me, but God intended it for good to accomplish what is now being done, the saving of many lives."* Jacob's misfortune eventually saved his family and his entire nation!

Along with the pain, 9/11 brought tremendous personal healing for many. Great things were and continue to be accomplished for the Kingdom from this act of evil. Chaplains were blessed to have been a small part in that healing. Over the years I have been a part of a Critical Incident Stress debriefing team. Whenever there is a traumatic incident like a police shooting, we helped by offering a program that let them know what they are experiencing is a normal reaction to an abnormal event. A question we ask toward the end of the process is, "What good has come out of this situation?" We usually get some puzzling looks but, as they think about it, there is a silver lining in the midst of the rubble. Quite often participants comment, "It brought us closer together as a team." And that is what I think happened at Ground Zero after 9/11. Thousands of volunteers poured in from around the nation, and even the world, to help. They lined the streets of the Westside Highway on the way to Ground Zero with signs greeting and encouraging us. They set up rest stations with food, chiropractors, baristas, podiatry nurses to take care of our feet, etc. Volunteers literally became the hands and feet of Jesus ministering to those who needed an encouraging example of hope.

This was a different event from a Columbine. Chaplain Steve Lee was the lead chaplain at Columbine.

He told me that, emotionally, Columbine was tougher on him than Ground Zero. There were no cheering crowds lining the streets leading to the school, no respite stations for the emergency workers. Different factions (police, fire, the school, administration, media, etc.) seemed to want to affix blame. One event brought us together while the other tore the community apart. Remember all of the American flags that were flying on 9/11 and afterwards? I went to my police department to check on our personnel and they already had flags attached to the patrol units flying in the breeze. The local flag company couldn't keep enough flags in stock. It's true that eventually, as we moved away from the event, fewer folks displayed their flags. At least for a while though, it brought national unity.

The ancient Greek philosopher Aristotle declared, "Nature abhors a vacuum." I grew up in a generation that remembers milk being delivered to our doors in glass containers. One of my favorite science experiments as a grade school student was to take a glass gallon milk bottle, light paper, and throw it in the container. I would then take a shelled hard-boiled egg and place it over the opening. As the flame consumed the oxygen it would burn out, creating a vacuum in the bottle. The air pressure on the outside would force the egg through the neck of the bottle making a deep "pop" sound as the egg dropped into the milk bottle.

The terrorists' destruction of the World Trade Center on September 11, 2001 created a vacuum in lower Manhattan, in New York City, and around this nation. As Aristotle observed, something had to fill the vacuum. Evil is always present so I'm sure the forces of the Enemy tried to invade that place with hatred and bitterness. But I believe, above all that, the forces of good crowded out the evil and secured a permanent residence at the WTC. Even now, as I write this, the freedom tower and memorial are being completed as a symbol of hope for all of us. In the end, hope is what filled the vacuum of Ground Zero. One only had to open one's heart to the hope and it would come rushing in like the egg falling into the milk bottle. Truthfully what happened at Ground Zero is what happens in every human heart. The devil brought the destruction of sin into our lives to destroy us. Just as there are scientific laws in place, such is the case in the spiritual world. The spiritual world hates a vacuum. Something must fill that void in our hearts. In the tenth chapter of St. John, we read about this spiritual battle between good and evil. It's the story of the sheep's gate. In New Testament times, at the end of the day, a shepherd would bring the flock of sheep into an area closed off by a short stone fence with one opening. The shepherd would then lie down in that opening, literally becoming a gate. In verses seven through ten of that chapter we read:

> 7 Therefore Jesus said again, "Very truly I tell you, I am the gate for the sheep. 8 All who have come before me are thieves and robbers, but the sheep have not listened to them. 9 I am the gate; whoever enters through me will be saved. They will come in and go out, and find pasture. 10 The thief comes only to steal and kill and destroy; I have come that they may have life, and have it to the full."

Satan, the ultimate terrorist, comes to steal, kill, and destroy. But if we follow Jesus, the shepherd and keeper of the gate, He will protect us and give us abundant life.

SENT TO SERVE...THE CHAPLAINS OF 9/11

The Cross found at Ground Zero

The only lasting solution to the problem of sin and evil in our lives is to replace it with the love of Jesus which fills the vacuum. The more we are filled with His love, the less room there is for evil. What greater hope can there be than the presence of God! May you open your heart to Him today and experience your own "Freedom Tower" in your heart.

One of the great symbols of hope at Ground Zero was the cross found two days after the attack in the Customs Building (World Trade Center #6). Frank Sileccia, a construction worker discovered the cross formed from structural steel by the collapse of the North Tower. A piece of sheet metal was wrapped over one arm that to some represented the Good Friday shroud. As Chaplain Steve Lee of Peace Officer Ministries put it, "The cross gave the appearance of a God-given sculpture in the middle of what was otherwise an amphitheater from hell." Steve went on to etch this poem in one of the cross arms:

From "God's House"
Fired new from dying flame,
This living sign remains,
Arms outstretched,
Embracing yet
Our avalanche of pain,
To still, to fill,
To heal again.

The cross is located a couple blocks from the World Trade Center at St. Peter's Catholic Church. The plan is to return it to World Trade Center when the museum opens in September, 2011.

Spiritual hunger was evident in our distribution of the "God's Word for Peace Officers" Bible. Everywhere we went the New York public safety personnel, from those in the precincts to those in the firehouses, dispatch centers, etc., were open to receiving a copy. We came up to some officers who were manning a barricade near Ground Zero. When we offered them a Bible one replied, "Thanks chaplains, but we really have no place to put it while on watch." Indicating we understood, we turned to walk away only to hear, "Wait chaplains, give me that Bible." The officer took it and smiled. I smiled too realizing that here was one of New York's finest standing in the street holding a copy of God's Word!

There was a place across the street from Ground Zero called Saint Joseph's Chapel.

Chaplains John Cundiff, Russ Guppy, and Wally Johnston at St. Joseph's Chapel on Liberty Street by Battery Park

St. Joseph's was a place where the rescue workers could get a hot meal, check email, and rest. We had a supply of the Bibles on hand there at all times. One young volunteer who was helping at the center enjoyed giving those Bibles to the workers. He would even carry a few in his backpack to give to someone when he was away from the center. He told us that a German camera crew came to the chapel. He spoke with them about the Bible so they had him hold one up so they could get a close up of the cover. They told him the cover of that Bible would be broadcast all over Germany that night! God's Word that offered hope to those in New York went international.

From Peace Officer Ministries, the producer of this special memorial edition of the Bible, posted this thank you note on their website:

> "I must thank you for the very generous donation of copies of "God's Word for Peace Officers" which were distributed to officers at Ground Zero and also to the family members of officers who died in the line of duty at the World Trade Center... Please convey my gratitude, on behalf of the New York City Police Department, to your colleagues at Peace Officer Ministries."

Chief Joseph J. Esposito, NYPD

> "Thank you for the copy of God's Word for Peace Officers... I appreciate your thoughtfulness, and I am grateful for your dedicated service to our nation. May God bless you, and may God continue to bless America."

President George W. Bush

I received the following note:

> "Wally...We are still talking about your visit and it was a bright moment in a very dark time for us here. The Bibles you gave us are a very visible reminder of your concern for us and I can't think of a room in our communications center that at least one of those Bibles isn't our on a desk at some point during each day. I know that I will always treasure my Bible for the warm wishes it represents."

Sgt. James V. Butler, N.Y.P.D. Communications Section (Dispatch)

While completing this book we received the news from President Obama that Osama bin Laden had been killed by our special forces. I was interviewed the following day, May 2, 2011, on a local Portland, OR radio station and asked my response. I replied "Guarded relief." Yes, the mastermind of 9/11 had been taken out but the war on terror continues. I went on to say,

> "I hope we will let this event bring us together similarly to 9/11. We were united if only for a few weeks or months. We have this habit of forgetfulness. We need to take such events and use them as a platform to unite us as one people fighting the war on terror."

The good that came out of the tragedy of 9/11 included the building of lifelong friendships, a spirit of volunteerism, and the response to the Word of God. All of these sent a message of hope to all who would hear.

For Your Consideration

Many don't know what to do each year on 9/11, also known as Patriot Day. For some it is too painful to remember. Others want to commemorate the day but don't know how. One positive idea is to help sponsor a 9/11 blood drive. We have done this the past few years at a local police department. A number of people told me, "I've never given blood before but I wanted to do something positive to remember 9/11. Thanks for doing this." We can remember those who died by giving the gift of life. Please contact your local chapter of the American Red Cross and your local police and/or fire department to set this up.

6 THE CHAPLAIN IN THE LOCAL COMMUNITY

The chaplain is a best kept secret in most communities. How they get their start can be as varied as there are communities. Some are career police or firefighters who want to continue to serve after retirement. Some come in contact with a public safety person in their church or social/community circle. They are invited to assist in some way and before they know it they are asked to be a chaplain. Chaplains have the "bug" and can't quite shake it. Many seemingly fall into the role but as time goes by they see God's hand in the whole affair. Some are called from a family of public safety service.

Most public safety chaplains are volunteers. They see chaplaincy as a part of their call from God. It is not a position that most young seminarians view as a possible career choice. It takes years of ministry in a community to build the clout and financial support before it can be called "employment." I often said that my wife worked to support my chaplain habit!

Chaplains generally work behind the scenes because most of their work is confidential. I tell people when they see a news story involving a crime or incident that affects officers or citizens, it would be a safe bet there is at least one chaplain working with those involved.

Police chaplains in your local community have a unique ministry setting. They are like roving social workers. They are involved with many people in different stages of need. They also rub shoulders with those in the community who can help meet the needs. They are a resource to form partnerships with citizens, city leaders, and the faith community.

This is illustrated in the story of Kim and Robert. I was called by dispatch about an infant boy who had died. When I arrived at the apartment, I met with some devastated parents. I spent a number of hours with them. During that time I asked their religious preference and other personal resources they might have. I tried to connect their needs to those resources. Kim told me they currently were not involved in church but had a background in a certain denomination. I said to them, "I know a good pastor in town from that denomination. Would you like for me to get into contact with him?"

"Oh yes, please do," they replied.

To make a long story short, that pastor and church showed love to that couple. Today they are a part of that congregation. After the death of their son they were headed for divorce but now have reconciled.

Quite often public safety chaplains become the "chaplain" for the pastors in their communities. Pastoring can be a lonely job. Pastors have few in whom they can confide. A chaplain becomes a safe place for them to share their personal needs and concerns for themselves and their congregations.

Often when I talk to groups I give my "Hat Speech." Chaplains wear various hats in their service to the community. Here are some of those hats:

<u>Counselor/Comforter:</u> Chaplains provide counseling for police/fire personnel and their family members as requested. They also offer referrals. Chaplains make notifications to households regarding the death of a family member. On a sunny Sunday afternoon I accompanied an officer to notify a mother of the sudden death of her son. He was a high school student on his way with friends to Disneyland when they were involved in a car crash. I was grieved to think that in a matter of moments my news would shatter this mother's life. She answered the door with a very bubbly personality. She asked us to wait until she put the dog in another room.

Once inside she asked, "So what brings you out here on a day like this?"

I replied, "I'm sorry to inform you that your son was killed in a car crash."

The response was immediate. She screamed and then grabbed for something on the coffee table. Fortunately she didn't throw anything at us. I'd learned to expect any response from fainting, anger, running to another room, etc. Over time she calmed down some until other family members started showing up. Each time she broke the news to someone in the family, the emotional reaction returned. The chaplain stays as long as the family desires and needs him/her. That can be anywhere from minutes, to hours, to days.

I've been asked, "How can you do this job?" I answer that I know I provide a needed source of comfort during the worst times of others' lives. Chaplains also provide assistance to the officers and firefighters who respond. They can hand off the families to us while they deal with the scene.

Patrol Partner: Chaplains ride along with officers during their patrol shifts. Most chaplains do some limited training along with the officers. Sometimes that even includes how to use the officer's weapons in case of emergencies. This helps the chaplain become less of a liability and more like a limited partner to the officer. Often the presence of a chaplain can calm a situation. While on patrol one evening, we noticed a large landscape truck parked in a red zone across from a bar. While the officer was calling for a tow truck, two big guys came barreling out of the bar. They were associated with the vehicle. These guys could have twisted us into pretzels. While one man was verbally confronting the officer, the other looked over at me. He saw the cross on my jacket and asked, "Are you a preacher, you know, like the kind that can marry people?"

I replied, "Yes."

He then turned to his partner and said, "Hey, cool it. This guy is a preacher!" That calmed them down so that we could safely take care of business.

Public Speaker: Chaplains are often asked to speak to civic groups, schools, churches, etc. They also represent their department and city at public safety memorial services, often as a speaker or participant in the program.

Social Worker/Community Networker: Chaplains help citizens in need to connect with available resources, whether food, housing, clothing, etc. Most chaplains are tied in with various social services. They often become the "go to" person in a community when needs arise. Chaplains can also act as catalysts to get community groups together. I belonged to a pastors' group that initiated Love In The Name of Christ (Love INC), in our community.

Love INC networks the churches together to meet the needs of the community. Chaplains often help to build partnerships in their communities to meet targeted needs.

Departmental Liaison: The chaplain becomes the liaison between the department and the community. Often chaplains become part of a ministerial group in the local community and work with churches on projects related to public safety. Community policing has become the standard in communities and it is about building partnerships with local law enforcement. Chaplains can play a vital role in helping to formulate such teamwork.

Educator: The chaplain is sometimes asked to teach at departmental citizen's academies. These are classes that train citizens on the operation of the police department. Many departments get their pool of volunteers from these academies. Many chaplains offer classes to new police and fire recruits and dispatchers covering topics like dealing with stress, relationships and communication.

A junior high student drowned just before the start of a new school year. I was asked to speak to the students and parents about how to work through the grief. I've been asked a number of times to offer that class to various groups.

Clergy: Chaplains provide clergy services such as weddings, baby baptisms, hospital visits, and funerals for both the department personnel and citizens. I was once called to a home where an infant died of natural causes. I helped the family walk through that experience. They asked me to provide a graveside service. I will never forget the little white casket and the pain I saw in the eyes of those present. Though it was difficult, I was grateful to provide some comfort to that devastated family.

Emergency Responder: Chaplains respond to local, state, regional, and national emergencies. Many are trained in "Critical Incident Stress Management" (CISM). CISM helps personnel to process their critical stress and get back on their feet to continue their work. An example of a critical incident is a police shooting, especially when a life is taken. Chaplains become part of a team that helps those involved work through their thoughts and emotions around that event. The difficulty with the rescue and recovery at Ground Zero was the length of the incident. The incident wasn't just the attacks on 9/11/01. The incident continued for those who worked on the "pile" at the World Trade Center. The attack and the rescue/recovery became one event lasting many months. This made it particularly difficult for the workers to handle.

I have often been asked, "Who takes care of the chaplains?" Self-care is an important need for chaplains. Unfortunately many chaplains are not good at the practice. Fortunately most chaplains have, if they seek it out, the opportunity of debriefing and unloading with other chaplains.

CONCLUSION

We end this book the way we started it—by talking about the heart of a volunteer.

The mission of The New York Says Thank You Foundation is to send volunteers from New York City each year on the 9/11 anniversary to help rebuild communities around the country affected by natural or man-made disasters as their way of commemorating the extraordinary love and generosity extended to New Yorkers by Americans from all across the United States in the days, weeks, and months following 9/11 (See www.newyorksaysthankyou.org).

One of the workers at Ground Zero said, "Don't ever forget these days boys. We came in as individuals and we walked out together." The events of 9/11 brought us together as a nation. Tragedy has a way of bringing people together. This time of trial brought me a new friend, NYPD Officer Arnold Chow. The night we left the dispatch center after handing out Bibles, we made our way across the street to visit the FDNY headquarters. The guard on duty that night was Officer Chow. After visiting with us for a while and seeing our credentials, he asked if we wanted to go inside and see the memorial wall. We later exchanged our cell numbers and we have been friends ever since. He and his family have visited us in Oregon and we stay with them when visiting New York City.

I hope you have found this book helpful in giving you, through the window of 9/11, a better understanding of and a new appreciation for what public safety chaplains do every day in your local community. I was privileged to have served as a chaplain for over 25 years. It was the greatest calling of my life and I feel I have benefitted as much as or more than the police officers in my departments. I have also had the wonderful privilege of working beside some great chaplains over the years who have modeled for me the role and spirit of the chaplain.

As I reflect on my experiences and those of my fellow chaplains during 9/11, I am reminded of a tribute paid to General Robert E. Lee, commander of the Confederate army during the American Civil War. Benjamin Hill, a contemporary of Lee, was a U.S. Senator. He shared this tribute to Lee which also captures the essence of what a public safety chaplain is about:

> "He was a foe without hate, a friend without treachery, a soldier without cruelty, and a victim without murmuring. He was a public officer without vices, a private citizen without wrong, a neighbor without reproach, a Christian without hypocrisy, and a man without guilt. He was Caesar without his ambition, Frederick without his tyranny, Napoleon without his selfishness, and Washington without his reward." [6]

---

[6] Senator Benjamin Hill's speech before the Southern Historical Society on February 18, 1874.

ABOUT THE AUTHOR

Wally Johnston's first published article appeared in a youth magazine in 1978. Since then he has written in various publications. His varied writing assignments have included feature articles, fillers, poetry, curriculum, devotionals, and newspaper articles.

He received his MA in Counseling Psychology from George Fox University and has been in private practice as a counselor/coach, and educator. He has taught in public and private schools and has been a police trainer.

Because Wally believes that relationships play a vital role in life, he established Foundations 4 Your Life in 2008. He provides relationship coaching and education.

Wally served 26 years as a law enforcement chaplain. He joined the International Conference of Police Chaplains in 1985 and has risen to its highest certification as a Master Chaplain.

You can reach Wally at:

Wally@Foundations4YourLife.com. You can also visit his website at: www.Foundations4YourLife.com. He would love to hear from you.

Made in the USA
Columbia, SC
08 July 2019